Life On Fire: A Step-By-Step Guide To Living Your Dreams

Kim Dinan

Life On Fire: A Step-By-Step Guide To Living Your
Dreams

Cover Design: Hannah Loaring, Further Bound Design

ISBN 978-1492397670

Acknowledgements

I have learned a serious lesson in the last year. The decision to write a book and the *act of writing it* are two completely different things. Without the support and encouragement of the following people I may still be stuck in the middle of the book writing process.

First and foremost, I would like to thank my husband Brian for his support and encouragement. No matter what big, crazy idea I come up with he always cheers me on. *Impossible* is not a word that this man has ever muttered. It's one of the many reasons that I love him.

Thank you to Mike and Terry Patton. Without your support I would not be living the life that I am today. You are an integral reason that my dream has come true.

Thank you to Michele and Glenn Crim for being the sort of upstanding humans that the world needs. You make me want to do you proud.

To my early readers Kelly Ross-Brown, Sarah Chamberlain, Wendy Gibson and Brian Patton who provided useful edits and suggestions and eagle-eyed proofreading, thank you.

Thank you to Granny who had to put up with me through the ups and downs of this book writing process.

Thank you to Hannah Loaring who created the beautiful cover design and other marketing pieces that helped me launch this book in style.

Finally, thank *you* for reading this book. It is my sincerest hope that when you close it for the final time you will feel ready to meet your dreams head on.

Life On Fire: A Step-By-Step Guide To Living Your Dreams

"The most powerful weapon on earth is the human soul on fire."
—Ferdinand Foch, French soldier and writer

Table of Contents:

Introduction: Shine

Hi, I'm Kim and I'm glad that you've found this book.

Before I dive into the heart of this book, I want to tell you a little bit about me. I am not a life coach or a psychologist. I do not have a degree in psychology (I studied literature in college). I cannot read tarot cards or guess the color of your chakra.

I am just a woman that decided, five years ago, to do something completely out of the ordinary. I decided to live my dream.

At the time, I was working as a Sustainability Coordinator for my local city government. I owned a house and a car and a matching set of plates and a closet full of clothes. I had a husband (still do!) and a backyard with a hammock and a flowerbed. I had the sort of life that you probably have now. But I also had something else. I had a constant, increasingly persistent voice inside of me that screamed at me like a madwoman, and I could not shut the damn thing up.

What had started as a nagging little whisper inside of my chest reminding me of my biggest dreams had grown, over the years, into an undeniable shout. As you might imagine, this screaming voice was entirely unwelcomed. I tried my best to ignore it, and I was successful for a while. But as time passed and the screaming grew louder, I eventually found I could no longer successfully silence the voice or shush it. The voice was determined not to be ignored.

The voice grew louder and louder. It wasn't a literal voice, like someone in the room with me, but an internal voice that spoke from within. The voice cried out for attention,

I ignored it, and so it began to manifest itself as crippling anxiety.

At work, where the voice would often boom the loudest, I developed the habit of taking a daily pilgrimage to the bathroom where I would lock myself into a toilet stall and talk myself down from panic attacks. The roaring voice, my *soul,* was screaming like a panicked child: *"KIM, THIS IS NOT WHAT YOUR LIFE IS FOR."*

It was, to steal a phrase from Al Gore, an inconvenient truth.

The thing was, I knew that working 9-5 in a cubicle for the local government was not *really* what my life was for. In fact, at some point earlier in my life I'd even believed that I was born to be a writer. But instead of writing or working with words, instead of even having a job in which I could be creative, I'd somehow found myself as a professional bureaucrat working 9-5 in a gray office cubical.

I'd also always dreamed of traveling the world. In my cubicle, I fantasized about exploring the far-off corners of Argentina or Nepal, of taking weeks or months to live in other countries and learn new languages and immerse myself in foreign cultures. I wanted to travel. I desperately wanted to write. But somewhere along the way I'd traded in my dreams for a pension and two weeks of annual vacation time.

I'd given up my dream, but then there was that roaring voice. The voice told me that my dream had not yet given up on me.

Let me step back a minute and say this: Until the voice of my soul started raging I could honestly say that I wasn't *that* unhappy. After all, life was easy. I was earning a good salary; I had a nice life where I could afford to do the things I wanted to do. Sure, I wasn't doing the thing that I felt I was born to do, but who was? Besides, I didn't believe it was possible or wise to just walk away from a career I'd invested ten years of my life in to pursue a career as a writer and a nomadic traveler. That was crazy-talk. I had a mortgage and a car and a life! Quitting my job to travel and devote myself to writing felt like quitting my job to pick daffodils for a living. Besides, I'd barely traveled outside of my own country and it had been years since I'd put a single creative word down on paper.

But there was the trouble of that unavoidable voice. That voice that had started as a prodding, questioning whisper, "Kim, don't you think that there's more you are here to do?" The voice that grew until it eventually screamed so loud I found myself at work, tucked into the bathroom stall, talking myself down from panic attacks. My soul was screaming at me to take a different path. My head told my soul it was impossible.

I will make this long introduction a bit shorter and tell you that after a few incredibly tough years, and after I tried almost everything in my power to silence my screaming inner voice, my soul won the battle. Over the course of three years I began writing, sold my house and all of my possessions, left my job, and set out into the world with my husband in order to write and travel.

I will forever be grateful for the incessant voice of my soul. My life is richer and fuller and filled with more possibility than it would have been had that voice kept quiet. I am on the path I was born to walk, but the process of getting here was confusing and scary.

That's where this book comes in.

Oftentimes people ask me, "How did you do it?" Other times, people tell me why they can't do it themselves. In the following chapters I will outline the process that I undertook to identify and follow my dreams. I hope that sharing this process will help you get started down the path towards truth and freedom in your own life. Our authentic truth is as unique as we are, but the path in which we honor that truth has been traveled before. This book will make the path of your own personal journey easier to navigate.

A few notes about the book

There is an argument, and I tend to agree with it, that not everyone needs to turn their dreams into their career. Some people are happy going to work as a bank teller and then coming home and writing their novel in the evenings. They don't need to quit their day job to chase their dreams. I acknowledge this method and applaud it. Do whatever fills you up and makes you happy in life.

Throughout this book I talk about living the life of your dreams as synonymous with earning an income doing what you love. This is because we spend so much of our time and energy earning an income that it makes sense for many of us to turn what we are here on earth to do into a living. As the poet Mary Oliver expressed it: "I simply do not distinguish between work and play." However, although I do sometimes mention earning money by offering your dreams as a service to the world, this book is not *only* about turning your dreams into your career.

This book is for you, whether you hope to earn an income through living your dreams or if you are happy maintaining your career and living your dreams outside of working hours. This book is for you no matter what your dream is, whether it is as quiet and true as learning to bring more calmness to your life or as big and bold as traveling the world. Whatever your dream, what matters is that we each allow the unique desire within our souls to see the light of day.

You will also find throughout this book that I use the term 'God' on a regular basis. I know that this is a polarizing word for many people and I want to make note of what I mean when I use the word.

God is the term I use to describe the greater force of energy that exists in the world. To you, God might be defined in Christian terms or in mystical terms. You might call God the universe, the divine spirit, a higher self, truth, or the great creator. Maybe God is in the Oak trees for you, or in your dog Norman or the still swamps of Florida. You do not need to have a concept of God at all to use this book. Please know that when I use the word God I am referring to whatever it is that *God means to you*, the greater force of life that brings you peace.

To get the most out of this book I recommend completing the exercises highlighted at the end of most chapters. I suggest designating a notebook specifically for these exercises and keeping it nearby as you read. You will use the notebook often. Feel free to record the thoughts and insights that enter your head as you are reading this book. The purpose of the notebook is to record your inner dialogue, your hopes and fears, and to help you make sense of your strongest desires.

I hope that by the end of this book you will feel inspired to take the next steps towards your truest life. There are tens of thousands of people embarking on the same sort of journey. You, yourself, must walk your path alone, but *you* are not alone. People are cheering for you. I am one of them.

I wish that this book had been written when I was at the very beginning of my own journey. It would have made the scariest parts of navigation a bit easier. But I know now that the reason it was not written before was because I had to write it myself. That's just one little thing that I learned along the way.

Shine,

Kim Dinan
www.so-many-places.com

A Preamble: Defining the life of your dreams

What does it mean to live your dreams? What would your life look like if you were, in fact, living your dreams?

Certainly the little phrase, "living your dreams," means different things to different people. I know quite a few people that might say, upon first response, that living the life of their dreams means buying the winning lottery ticket, moving into a mansion, hiring a butler, collecting foreign cars and taking elaborate luxury vacations.

That sounds sort of nice.

But upon closer inspection I suspect those people will admit that even all of the money in the world, a life of absolute luxury, would not truly make them happy if they are not also fulfilled and excited about life.

Money will make you rich on the outside but living your dream is the real source of wealth.

_____

Naming the life of my dreams

When I acknowledged the voice inside of me and began seriously considering my dream, I thought long and hard about what it meant for me to live the life of my dreams. What did I really want? What did my soul long to do? I realized that the life of my dreams meant doing the thing that fills me up inside: writing. It meant having the time and energy to connect with the people that matter in my life. It meant having control over my schedule so that I could travel and see the world. It meant having room in my day to exercise. It meant being outside when I wanted to be outside. It meant making soup and banana bread on a Wednesday afternoon if I felt like it.

I determined that the life of my dreams was to earn enough income through writing, the thing that fills me up, so that I didn't have to spend 40-hours a week or more doing something that empties me.

And I didn't need a million dollars to begin living the life of my dreams. I could begin now.

The life of your dreams may be similar or vastly different than my own. But before we begin talking about the concrete steps that I took to live my dreams, and how you can take your own, you must first define what the life of your dreams looks like to you.

———————

Preamble Exercise

Describe the life of your dreams

Take out your notebook and write down what a single day of your life would look like if you were living your dreams. Think about what time you would get up, what you would eat, who you would spend your day with, what you would do for work, and where you would live. Think over every detail of your day and write it down.

Remember that there is no winning lottery ticket. You must earn an income like everyone else. You must still pay your bills and get the kids off to school and eat three times a day. The everyday aspects of life still exist. But how would your day be structured if you were living the life of your dreams?

Would you have breakfast with your family? Would you head off to your dream job (make sure to define your dream job) or work for yourself from home? Who would you see during your day? Would you exercise? Walk the dog? Do yoga? Go swimming in the ocean?

Make sure you list the crucial components of your happiness.

Some things to consider:

- Where does your perfect day take place? What country? What environment? Would you be near the mountains? The ocean? The great, sweeping plains?

- How would you break up the hours in your day? How many hours would you work? Sleep? Socialize? Exercise? Play with the kids?

- What do you need to do each day to fill yourself up? Do you need quiet time? Time to write or paint? Time to talk with your partner? Time to read a book?

- What would you eat? Would you cook at home?

- What would you do for work? Where would you work? Who would you work for? Who would you work with?

Have you done it? Good. Make sure you keep your notebook at hand so you can look back on what you've written later.

For now, though, spend a minute identifying the themes in your answer and write those down as well. Does your perfect day include spending more time alone or with your family? Is it drastically different then the life you are living now? Does it involve spending more time outdoors or more focused time on your passion?

Defining what the life of your dreams will actually look like *in real life* is the crucial first step to turning your dreams into reality.

Remember, in order to get what you want out of life you must first know what you want.

Chapter 1: The voice inside

"When you can't go forward, and you can't go backward, and you can't stay where you are without killing something deep and vital in yourself, you are on the edge of creation."
—Sue Monk Kidd, author

"Listen—are you breathing just a little and calling it life?"
—Mary Oliver, poet

We all have a voice that speaks inside of us. More often than not this voice is a critical voice, a voice that chastises us for eating another cookie or daydreaming on the job when we should be working. This voice of negativity is the voice that speaks from inside of our heads.

But we also have a deeper voice that we are capable of accessing. It's a voice that speaks the truth. This voice, the voice of our soul, knows when we are not being honest with ourselves. This voice doesn't let us get away with the excuses we tell ourselves in order to put off our dreams.

Many of us try very hard to silence this voice in our lives because it is hard to hear the truth, especially when the truth is telling us that we want something drastically different than what we currently have. The voice of our soul feels very dangerous to those of us unused to letting it speak.

When you are on the verge of making a big transition in your life, or if you are thinking of doing something out of the ordinary, something risky, something that excites you but scares the bejesus out of you, the voice in your head will pepper you with all kinds of reasons why you cannot do the thing your soul wants you to do.

Your soul: I would like to submit my poetry to the local poetry contest.

Your head: Why waste your time? You'll never win.

Your soul: I would like to ask that interesting woman on my soccer team out to lunch.

Your head: She has other things to do, why would she want to become friends with you?

Your head will throw fear and negativity and your deepest and darkest insecurities at you in order to talk you out of listening to the voice of your soul. Your head will try to talk you out of almost everything that the voice inside of your soul is trying to talk you in to.

Many people, when they consider pursuing their dreams, hear the negative voice inside of their head and they stop. They become paralyzed by fear. They let their head call the shots. But if you want a direct connection to the truth, you have to move past the voice in your head and listen to the voice of your soul.

Identifying the voice of your soul

If you are at the beginning of your journey and are not yet used to honing in to the voice of your soul, then it is likely that you don't hear this voice speak very often. The voice inside of your head is your dominant voice.

Perhaps the voice of your soul slips out in a dream or in a rare moment while you are showering or driving down the Interstate. In those moments of vulnerability or distraction, the voice inside of your soul finds a way to sneak out, "I wanted to be a songwriter!" it screams.

It's a shocking moment when the voice of your soul first speaks. Oftentimes, too sad or stunned by the emergence of the voice of our soul, we stifle it as quickly as possible. Then the voice inside our head rushes in to clean up the mess, hushing the voice in our soul with sensible and realistic thoughts about how we could never have made it as a songwriter. The voice in our head reminds us that adults with responsibilities have to give up unrealistic dreams like that.

This is how the voice of the head suffocates the voice of the soul.

It is not our fault. We have been taught to dismiss the voice in our soul and trust only the voice in our head. The media, society, school and our parents drill the concept into us. We are taught to "use our head." We are taught to "think things through." We are taught to be cautious and regimented. But what have we been taught about the soul? When have we been encouraged to do something, learn something, or try something just because it excites us? Where does passion come in?

We are sometimes taught to "listen to our gut" or "trust our instincts" but usually only in situations in which we may find ourselves in danger. Isn't it interesting that in situations when we really need clarity, in situations that may even mean the difference between life and death, that only then are we taught to listen to the voice of our soul?

Why shouldn't we listen to our gut or trust our instincts when we are making decisions about what we should do with our life? And I'm not just referring to making the decision about what we will do as a career. I mean, *what we will do with our life* and how we will invest our precious, fleeting hours. By believing that we must be sensible and listen to our head when our soul is crying out for something different, we lose the part of us that is uniquely put inside of us by God (or the universe, the divine spirit, the great energy, your spirit animal or whatever it is that *God means to you*). The voice of our soul is our own private telephone line to God. So when we silence the voice of our soul and let our head take over, we muddle the connection. This is how our biggest gift, our direct connection with our soul and therefore to God, is stifled.

Let me explain how it happened to me. I was born to be a writer. I know this because as a young child I spent hours alone in my room writing poems. No one taught me how to do this; it was just a form of expression that came out of me. Poetry was a thing that came naturally and made me come alive.

I wrote all through my childhood and when it was time to choose what I would go to college to do I told my parents I wanted to be a writer. "You don't need to go to school to be a writer," said my parents. "Why don't you go for Journalism?" So I applied for Journalism school and when I didn't get in I settled on English where I could at least read books and take a poetry writing class or two.

I was a mediocre student but I excelled at my major. I was especially good at my creative writing classes. My teachers would pull me aside and encourage me to go to graduate school, get an MFA and focus on my writing.

"Maybe I'll go to graduate school for writing?" I said to my parents.

"You don't need to go to graduate school to be a writer," they said. "The likelihood of making a living as a writer is very small. You should choose a career where you will make money. You want to be able to support yourself, don't you? If you really want to write, you can do that in your free time."

And because I did not think to question the logic, I accepted that I could not both do what I was born to do and be successful at it. So I found a career working for the local government.

It didn't take long before I stopped writing poems. Whether I wanted it to or not, my "successful" career was forcing my dream to take a back seat in my life. I found that I was too tired in the evenings after a full day of work to come home and be creative.

After a while I even stopped writing in my journal. For eight years I did not write at all. And during those years the part inside of me that was the most alive, the writer in me, withered into the tiniest of balls. For eight years I walked around not fully alive, the brightest and best parts of me had fallen dormant.

I was not writing anymore and there was a deep, gaping hole in my soul. But my parents were proud of me, society seemed to smile upon me, and I felt like I was the textbook model of success. "Just be happy!," my head told my soul. "Why can't you just be satisfied with your life? Why do you always want more?" My head pounded this rhetoric into me, saying whatever it had to say to keep my soul from speaking up.

For eight years I ignored my dream. Every once in a while the voice of my soul would pop to the surface when I had a quiet moment alone with myself. In those rare moments I knew, deep down, that there was a hollow place inside of my soul. But I filled that space with other things: Sports and happy hours and decorating my newly purchased home. I filled the emptiness by keeping myself busy. For a while it seemed like that might just work.

But as the years went by, the voice inside my soul began to speak louder. I tried to shut it up, but each time I stuffed the voice away my anxiety increased. I knew the truth, but I could not bear to admit the truth. I knew that I was unfulfilled inside, but I felt that at this point in my life accepting what I already had was my only option. I'd resigned myself to living a life that wasn't completely satisfying.

And that was when my soul began screaming in a desperate effort to be recognized.

I wrote a poem a few years ago about the moment I finally listened to the voice of my soul. Here is an excerpt:

> One day a voice inside me said:
> Kim, this is not what your life is for.
> And, against the odds, I listened.
> I said, "Well, what is it for?"
> And the voice said, "You know."
> The voice said it softly, because she knew I was afraid.
> She said, "You know, sweet honey love baby. I don't need to tell you."

You have a voice too. We are all born with this voice. It is the voice of our truest self. It is the voice of God speaking through us. It is a voice that will not guide us wrong.

Maybe your dream is not to write. Maybe it is to take care of animals or bake cupcakes or design beautiful clothing or travel the world. It does not matter what your dream is. If you have turned your back on your dream then I know that you will relate to my story. Perhaps you have felt similar feelings of emptiness and anxiety.

But once you recognize the voice of your soul and are truthful with yourself, the voice in your soul will no longer be an enemy but a trusted friend.

Move beyond the voice in your head and listen to the voice in your soul.

The question is now: How do I move beyond the cynical voice in my head and access the voice of my soul?

The first step to accessing the voice of your soul is to ask your soul to speak up. Perhaps your soul has been quiet for so long that you will ask it to speak and nothing will come out. Keep asking. As your soul flexes its vocal chords eventually you will hear it peep. Say to your soul, "What's that? I can barely hear you." Ask your soul what it wants. Ask and ask and ask until you hear the answer. And then continue to talk to your soul and wait patiently for your soul to talk back.

A good way to practice this is when you need to make a minor decision. For example, say that you must choose whether to stay in for the evening or go out with friends. To practice communicating with your soul, ask it what it would prefer to do. Close your eyes, get quiet, and ask. Your soul might tell you it would like to stay in and read a book. It might tell you it wants to go dancing with friends. Eventually, you will become so practiced at communing with your soul that you will be able to access the voice, tap into it, and talk to it whenever you need to. This comes in handy when you are faced with big decisions.

I get dozens of emails a week from people seeking advice. They say, "I really want to teach ballet for a living but my husband doesn't support it. I don't know what I should do." And I tell them the same thing my soul told me: "You do know what to do. You already know the truth. You carry the truth inside of you. *Listen.*"

I once read somewhere that the truth taps you on the shoulder. If you ignore her she'll stomp on your toes. Ignore her still? She'll punch you in the gut. Finally, she'll whack you over the head, repeatedly, until you finally pick yourself up one day, bruised and bloody, and ask, "Why have I been ignoring the truth for so long? I've known about her ever since she tapped me on the shoulder."

Find the voice of your soul and let it speak.

———————

Chapter 1 Exercise

Allow your soul to speak

Pull out your notebook and write this sentence at the top of the page:

What my soul wants more than anything is…

Now ask yourself, out loud, what you want. For example, I will say out loud to myself, "Kim, what do you want more than anything?" It is powerful to hear your own voice asking this question aloud.

Now spend twenty minutes free-writing your answer. Don't force or edit the responses that flow from your pen. Don't correct typos or try to filter the thoughts and ideas as they emerge. Just write, write, write. Allow your soul the chance to speak.

———————

Chapter 2: What were you born to do?

"There is no greater gift you can give or receive than to honor your calling. It's why you were born. And how you become most truly alive."
—*Oprah Winfrey, talk show host and philanthropist*

"Everyone has been made for some particular work, and the desire for the work has been put in every heart."
—*Rumi, 13ᵗʰ century poet*

I regularly receive emails from people that write to say, "Kim, I really admire what you are doing and I'd like to do something similar, but I don't know what I want to do with my life."

To which I respond with some iteration of a sentiment originally shared by Oprah Winfrey:

"If you don't know what your passion is, realize that one reason for your existence on earth is to find out."

You can begin to identify your purpose in life by honing in on what feels right and natural to you and what feels inauthentic. Maybe you feel absolutely yourself when you are hiking in the forest, or caring for stray cats, or babysitting. Understand that this feeling of naturalness is a sign that you are close to something that you were born to do.

Deep down we all know what makes us come alive. It may have been a very long time since we have done the thing that makes us come alive, but we have all had moments of divineness and clarity when we know we are doing something that fills us up. For example, I felt this way when I went on my first overnight backpacking trip as a freshman in college. Being deep in the wilderness made me feel alive in a way I'd never felt before. I knew from that moment on that I needed to make room in my life for wild spaces.

What has brought you the same sort of clarity? What has brought you the same feeling of sureness and aliveness?

When you are trying to determine what you were born to do, ask yourself what you would do if you felt that you were able and free to do anything in the world with a guarantee that you would not fail. Many times, our fear of failure is so great that it blocks us from acknowledging our true purpose.

Perhaps you can't recall off the top of your head what you would do if you could do anything because it has been so long since you've considered the notion. Start considering the notion today. I have never met a single person that doesn't know what they love. It might be a general sentiment: I love animals, I love making people laugh, and I love gardening. Pay attention to those things. Those things are where you start.

I am going to make a wild declaration: You know what you are here to do. What you don't know is the way to get there. You love to make people laugh. Making people laugh makes you come alive. So how do you build a life with that passion at your center? That is the part you don't know.

I use the words "passion" and "purpose" interchangeably because what you are here on earth to do, your purpose, is to come alive and to bring the world more alive with your vibrancy. Your passion is what you were born to do.

Your passion is the string that reaches from God's hand to you here on earth. Your passion connects you to the divine.

Cary Tennis said in his amazing advice column for *Salon*, "Your destiny may not be some world-shattering discovery. Your destiny may be something quiet and true, but you will know it. It won't make you insecure. It will come with a kind of 'aha' feeling, and a sigh of contentment."

Passion. Destiny. Purpose. They're all names for one essential idea: To know why you are here, to do the thing that lights you up, to live as though you are on fire.

———————

How do I find my passion?

For those of you who have not found your passions yet or who need help rediscovering them, here are a few tips to help you identify them.

Tip 1: What did you love to do as a child?

One way to begin to identify what you are here on earth to do is to think about what you loved to do as a child. Did you love to read, build Lego castles, dig in the mud and study bugs? Did you love to write poems at sunset or help your parents prepare dinner? Did you love walking in the forest and listening to the call of the birds?

Identify what made you come alive as a child. This is an important clue into where your passions lie. As children, we are unencumbered by expectations. We do what we love simply because we love it. These things that we love are our passions, born inside of us just like our bones. As children we shine, we do what comes naturally, and we do what we love.

When we are young we are asked, "What do you want to be when you grow up?" And when we respond, "I want to be a painter!" Our parents laugh and say, "Oh, no she doesn't. She's going to be a lawyer!" As children we hear in our parents voice that a lawyer is a respected profession that will make them proud but a painter is not. That is when the seed of *what life should be* is planted deep into our minds. In this way we are conditioned over the years to believe that a lawyer is a valuable thing to be and a painter is not.

The child that we were we still are. Think back to what you loved as a child, this is a clue into what your soul still loves.

Tip 2: What do people tell you that you are good at?

When you were young, what did people tell you that you were good at and how did this influence your life? Perhaps hearing adults tell you what you were good at encouraged and pushed you along towards your natural passions and inclinations? Or, perhaps it dragged you away from them. You loved to draw and design clothing but your parents or teachers insisted that your true abilities lie in math. So you became an accountant.

Your friends always tell you that you are a good listener. They come to you with their problems and you are proud of the fact that they trust you with their emotions. You feel comfortable helping them and filling this role brings you joy. Pay attention to these feelings and the nudges that come from your friends in the form of compliment. The satisfaction and ease at which you fulfill roles are clues to your calling.

Tip 3: What do you desire?

Some people say to me, "Kim, I don't know what I was born to do." And when I ask them what they want to do they say, "Well, I work in marketing now but I'd really like to be a social worker." Well, *hello*, that is what you were born to do.

So many people do not realize that what they desire to do is also what they were born to do. The aspiring social worker was given the desire to help her fellow humans because she has been put on earth to help. She has been given a soul of compassion and an assignment by God to make the world a kinder place for those that are struggling. Sure, it may not be as wild as wanting to dance the jig for the rest of her life, but it is her unique calling. Don't discredit or underestimate what you desire to do.

I know what I was born to do but I don't know how to do it

There is another sub-set of people who know what they were born to do but don't know how to set their dreams in motion. To these people I must first say, *congratulations!* Not only do you know what you were born to do, but you have actually "admitted" that you were born to do it.

I use the word "admitted" because I remember how terrifying it was for me to allow myself to recognize the fact that I knew what I was put on earth to do.

Deep down I knew what I was here to do (remember, my soul was screaming it) but for a long time I was too afraid to actually say it aloud. Admitting that I knew I was put on earth to write was an incredibly bold statement for a girl who studied spreadsheets at work, sat by the photocopier, and hadn't lifted a pen in years. I worried I sounded crazy. I worried I would be judged. And I felt incredibly vulnerable. How embarrassing if I failed after making such a bold claim.

It is a paralyzing feeling to know what you are here to do but to not know how to begin doing it. Sometimes, the truth of "not knowing how to do it" is actually a case of "too afraid to do it." We will discuss this more in Chapter 3: Getting Started and Chapter 5: Fear and Obstacles.

If you are currently living with the truth of your dream but not yet taking actions towards living that dream, you may feel as if you are letting yourself down or you may feel that life is passing you by. Don't worry. By admitting your dreams you have already taken the first steps towards living them. **It is never too late to begin living the life you are meant to live.**

We will talk more about the process of turning your dreams into reality in the following chapters.

Once, back in my government job, I sat through a lecture by an Entomologist who was so incredibly jazzed up and in love with the bugs that he studied that I was on the edge of my seat listening to him. For an hour and a half I barely breathed while he spoke of insect behavior and natural ecosystems. Bugs weren't exactly a subject that I cared anything for, but seeing this man's world through his eyes and hearing his excitement and love for these creatures made me feel like I'd stuck my finger in an electrical socket. I left that lecture knowing that I was in the presence of someone who was doing exactly what he was put on earth to do.

We all want to be the bug guy. Do not stop looking for the thing that fills you up until you have found your bugs.

———————

Chapter 2 Exercises

What did you love to do as a child?

Open to a blank page in your notebook. At the top of the page write the following:

Things I loved to do as a child.

Now begin to create a list. What were your favorite toys and games? Where did you play? Did you love to read or dig in the dirt or somersault? If you are in contact with someone who knew you when you were young, ask your elder what it was you loved to do. Assemble a list of the things you loved to do and add to this list when a new memory strikes.

What do you excel at?

Take out your notebook. At the top of the page write this sentence:

I know that I am good at...

1.
2.
3.
4.
5.
6.
7.
8.
9.
10.

After you have listed 10 things that you are good at (running, baking cupcakes, public speaking, painting nails) spend fifteen minutes free-writing about all of the ways you were influenced in your life as they relate to these ten things. What directions were you pushed in? What did your influencers tell you that you were good at? What did they tell you that you were bad at? What stories have you been telling yourself about yourself? What did you feel you had to prove and how has that impacted your life? Make a list. Write it all down.

———————

Chapter 3: Getting started

"The one thing all famous authors, world class athletes, business tycoons, singers, actors, and celebrated achievers in any field have in common is that they all began their journeys when they were none of these things."
—Mike Dooley, entrepreneur and writer

"There comes a time when one must risk everything or sit forever with ones dreams."
—Author unknown

Whether you've acknowledged your dream and are ready to act on it or you're just ready to find and listen to the voice in your soul, this chapter will help you get started.

It is completely normal to feel that your dream is the biggest, scariest, insurmountable goal in the world. For one thing, if your dream were easy to pursue you would have already done it by now!

But the primary reason that you have not tackled your dream is because it matters so much to you. We fear that if we fail at the one thing that matters we will have nothing left. We understand that it is one thing to fail at something that we do not care much about and another thing completely to fail at something that matters more than anything. I understand the resistance and the fear to get started. I've been there myself.

Let's say that your dream in life is to run an outdoor wilderness camp for children. You have never worked with children before. You don't have any wilderness training. In fact, you don't even work outdoors. You work in a cubicle and you wear a tie to work. You love the wilderness more than anything, you come completely alive out there, and you want to give that gift to children. This is your *dream*. But where do you start?

You have to start where everyone starts: At the beginning.

Start at the beginning and start small. Take it one step at a time. Start by signing up for a local class on wilderness survival skills. Start by volunteering at a local camp. Start by hiking more and spending more time doing what you love. When you do that you will meet other people that love what you love and a few of those people might actually do what you love for a living.

Start by reading books. Start by gathering information. Give yourself over to your dream. Put your energy into the direction of your goals and that energy will begin to pay off for you. Perhaps not in the way you expect, because you cannot go into this process expecting anything. You go into this process because you absolutely have to act, because your truest potential will not be realized if you do not set the wheels in motion.

Start by simply focusing your thoughts and ideas towards the achievement of dream. Start by listening to the way you talk. Do you say, "If I ever open a wilderness camp," or do you say, "When I open a wilderness camp"? This stuff matters.

Read this book and other books like it. Do research on your dream. Tell the people that you love and trust about your dream.

The steps at first are small; they're about shifting the energy around you. They're about changing what you believe yourself to be; they're about laying the foundation so that when challenging times come and you have to fight hard for your dream, you'll have the inner strength to keep the dream alive.

Reach out to people who are doing what you want to be doing. Chances are that these people will welcome you and encourage you because they, too, once started from the beginning.

There will come a time for a big gesture. You will have to take a major risk, eventually, to get your dream off of the ground. And you will know when that time has come. But for now, when you are getting started, begin with the small things. Start by changing the way that you think and act and the way that you talk to yourself. Start by making decisions today that are in line with the life you want to live five years down the road. Don't buy seven new three-piece suits if you plan to leave the office. Go on an outdoor leadership course as your vacation. Put the wheels in motion.

When I was just starting on the long road to my own dream, there was a quote by Martin Luther King, Jr. that I constantly recited to myself. It reminded me that I did not have to have a detailed roadmap to success and that I did not have to know every single action that I was going to take along the way. It reminded me that I just had to take it one step at a time:

"You do not have to see the whole staircase, just take the first step."

Do not get caught up in the fear of not knowing what to do next. What to do next is none of your concern right now. Your concern is what to do *now*.

At the end of this chapter you will be asked to compile a list of 10 concrete things you can do right now to get your dream rolling. Start walking towards your dream by conquering the first thing on your list. Never mind how much you resist it, how dumb you think it is, how small it feels, how scary it is. Do it anyway. Commit yourself, and watch your world change before your eyes. Do the first thing. When the first thing has been done sufficiently the next thing will appear.

Act as though you are driving a car through a blizzard in which you cannot see more than fifteen feet in front of you. Go slowly, stay focused, move forward into the space you can see and know that, when you get there, another fifteen feet will be illuminated for you. You have to trust the process.

There are no shortcuts. You can't hop from the seventh step to the tenth. You have to take them one by one. Remember, you will never see the whole staircase but you will always see the next step. It will appear right when you need to see it.

So you're like, "Okay, Kim, that sounds great and all but *what is the first step?*"

Guess what? You've already taken it. Acknowledging that there is something greater that you should be doing, a dream that exists inside of you that needs tending, *that* is the first step. The first step is telling the truth and listening to the voice of your soul. And one more bonus piece of good news: *That* step, the one in which you are truthful with yourself for perhaps the first time in your life, is the hardest of all.

My staircase

When I was in my early 20's I was very overweight and I committed myself to losing weight and becoming a healthier person. At that point in my life I was also a smoker. My eating habits were terrible. My exercise routine was nonexistent. I was 23 and my blood pressure was high.

I lived about a mile away from a gym and for months before I ever stepped foot in that gym, every time I drove past it I said to myself, "That is the place that I will go to get in shape." I was mustering up the courage to do it.

I remember one day I was in the car with a friend. We drove past the gym and I said to him, "In January I am going to join that gym and get into shape."

"That's great," he said. He was supportive, of course, but mostly uninterested.

At work I would read exercise blogs. I would print out healthy recipes and stick them into a book I kept in my kitchen. I tried to think like a fit person. What small changes could I make in my life?

Just as I'd proclaimed to my friend in the car a few months earlier, at the start of the New Year I joined the gym. I knew that there was a lot contributing to my weight gain and a lot of things that I would have to focus on in order to lose weight for good. I needed to be more active, I needed to change my diet, I needed to quit smoking, I needed to confront some of the things that were eating me from the inside (not a small one was the fact that I was not following my dreams!). I knew that there were many things that I would have to take on over time in order to be a healthy person, but right now I knew that I could only take the first step. The first step for me was joining the gym. I knew that if I tried to tackle all of the steps at once I would fail, but if I just concentrated on the first step the journey would be more manageable.

So I started going to the gym. I was the unhealthiest person at the there! I was so embarrassed in my spandex shorts, but I did not let my embarrassment stop me. I knew I was in the place I needed to be.

I went to the gym every day. Even on the days when it was the last thing on earth that I wanted to do. I went and after a certain amount of time I actually enjoyed going. I was feeling better every day, slowly losing weight, and my fitness was increasing by leaps and bounds. I was still smoking and I was still eating whatever I wanted, I wasn't yet focusing on those areas of my life. But what I found was that as I became more fit by going to the gym, and I began feeling better overall, I wanted to eat better.

The next step had appeared.

So I began focusing on my diet, making simple changes, choosing foods that made me feel healthy when I ate them. And as my fitness continued to improve and my diet began to improve, I started looking like a new person. I barely recognized my body in the mirror. I was beginning to be the kind of healthy person I knew I could be. But I also knew that it was time to face a hard truth: That even though I was exercising and eating well, I could never consider myself a healthy person if I was smoking.

The next step appeared again.

It was time to stop smoking. So I stopped smoking. It was not easy. But I had confidence that I was able to do things that weren't easy. After all, I'd carried my butt to the gym every day these past five months, hadn't I? I'd stuck to a commitment I'd made to myself. I was transforming myself physically. I had the power to stop smoking too.

If I had attempted to stop smoking at the same time I

began working out at the gym, I would have failed. If I had declared that all of a sudden I was going to go to the gym every day, eat a 1,800-calorie all-natural diet, and never smoke a cigarette again, I wouldn't have lasted the day. But because I took it step-by-step, I was able to achieve my goal in manageable parts.

Eventually I lost 80 pounds and became a marathon runner. I'd never have anticipated that I would have started running but one day that step appeared in front of me. I said to myself, "It's a nice day, Kim. Why not go outside and try running?" It was hard and terrible but when it was over I felt great. I became a runner. Running was the next step.

Running lead me to have an even greater belief in myself and in what I was able to do. Running gave me confidence in myself. It was during a trail run, one day while deep in the forest, that I stopped and listened to that inner voice that had been screaming at me for so long. It was during a run that I stopped and let the voice of my soul say out loud for the first time, "Kim, this is not what your life is for."

Each step that I took in my life lead to the next step, but I am not sure how it would have all turned out if I had not dragged my butt to the gym all of those years ago. The first step is getting started. We cannot know exactly where the staircase will lead us, but know for sure that important things will begin to happen *the second* you take the first step.

———————

Chapter 3 Exercise

Take action towards your dream

Take out your notebook and write down 10 concrete actions that you can take right now in order to work towards your dream. For example, if your dream is to own a wilderness camp your list may look like this:

10 things I can do to pursue my dream of owning a wilderness camp:

1. Write my dream on a piece of paper and display it on my desk.
2. Find out when the next hiking club meeting is and attend it.
3. Research nearby wilderness camps. Set up a meeting with the owners.
4. Obtain wilderness rescue certification.
5. Take CPR and first aid class at local Red Cross.
6. Research educational credentials I will need.
7. Pursue part-time job at wilderness camp to gain experience.
8. Study my financials. Determine financial decisions I will need to make in order to fund a camp.
9. Research how to write a business plan. Begin writing business plan.
10. Read books by others who have opened a wilderness camp. How did they start?

Hang your list on your refrigerator, above your computer monitor, or somewhere visible where you will see it every day. Begin working towards checking the 10 things off of your list. As a few tasks are completed add new tasks to the list.

Chapter 4: Noticing the universe

"What you seek is seeking you."
—Paulo Coelho, writer

"There are only two ways to live your life. One is as though nothing is a miracle. The other is as though everything is a miracle."
—Albert Einstein, physicist

Once you begin to take the first few steps towards your dream, you will notice an uncanny thing: The universe will conspire to help you.

Really.

This is because the universe responds to the energy that you put out into it. The universe wants you to succeed in living your dreams because when you live your dreams you make the universe a bigger and better place. And the universe likes to build its army of those that live from the soul whenever it possibly can. The universe is always recruiting.

Keep your eyes open for the signs you receive from the universe. What does not initially seem like a sign might actually be one. Really pay attention. The people you meet, the things you read on the Internet, or the catalog that is accidentally mailed to your house might all be messages from the universe.

———————

Signs from the universe on my own journey

Months after I'd admitted my dream, rearranged my life and left my home and job in the United States to travel and write, I found myself on a mountaintop in Chile.

It had been a rough few months. My husband and I had been traveling through South America at warp speed and were exhausted. It was nearing the holidays and we were homesick. We desperately wanted to go home for Christmas but we had already purchased plane tickets to India, our next destination.

I was headed to India to partake in an event called The Rickshaw Run in which I would be driving a motorized three-wheeled rickshaw 3,500 kilometers (2,175 miles) through the country. I was terrified. I was questioning everything. The Rickshaw Run felt like a death wish.

I was feeling scared, tired and defeated. I just wanted to go home and spend the holidays with my family. This whole traveling thing hadn't turned out quite like I expected.

But here I was on this mountaintop in Chile, so far away from home. I was with my husband and a few of our friends. We were hiking the "W" in Chile's Torres del Paine National Park, a popular wilderness backpacking route in Chile's Patagonia region.

As I hiked I found myself silently thinking over my options. Should I go home or should I go to India? The old feelings of fear and doubt ran through my head. The easy thing, I knew, would be to just book one-way tickets home. But I felt that there was something in India, too, and that if I could just push through this barrier of homesickness and fear that India might have something to offer me.

As these thoughts were running through my head I stopped with my hiking partners on the top of a rocky clearing to take in the view of the hauntingly blue Glacier Gray. We stood on a pristine overlook, admiring the panorama, when my friend kneeled down and pulled from the rocky scree a silver OM symbol on a broken black string. OM is an ancient mantra of Hindu Indian origin. It is represented by a single symbol that my friend had plucked from the ground.

I was stunned. The chances that this necklace would fall in this spot and that my friend would see it and wordlessly hand it to me as I was questioning my decision to travel to India seemed impossibly low. I'd never received such a strong message from the universe in my life.

I took the message (Universe, I hear ya!) and I went to India. India transformed me from the inside. It transformed my writing and it transformed my life. But that is for another book.

I don't believe in coincidences. That OM symbol was a pretty obvious message from the universe, but the second that I decided to start living my dreams I received dozens of other messages as well. In the most amazing fashion the universe recognized that I was making efforts towards my dream and began to conspire to help me live it.

Some signs that you receive from the universe will be big (like the OM symbol) and others will be small. Sometimes they will be as simple as a kind email or word that will lift your spirits when you are feeling down. All around you the universe is sending you signs, but it is up to you to recognize them.

You might not totally understand the meaning of a sign from the universe until after the fact, sometimes years later. Steve Jobs verbalized this sentiment quite well:

"You can't connect the dots looking forward; you can only connect them looking backwards. So you have

to trust that the dots will somehow connect in your future. You have to trust in something- your gut, destiny, life, karma, whatever. Because believing that the dots will connect down the road will give you the confidence to follow your heart even when it leads you off the well-worn path; and that will make all the difference."

—*Steve Jobs, entrepreneur and inventor*

Sometimes the reasons for a thought, action, or turn of events are not obvious at the time. Just have faith that those reasons will be revealed to you in due time. Patience is part of this path.

If you give yourself over to your dream, the universe will back you up. The universe will be on your team, sending you messages and clearing roadblocks from your path.

Keep your eyes open for signs, which may appear in both big and small ways. And rest assured that when something unbelievable happens (you find your OM symbol) or when you receive a little pick me up just when you need it (a kind email arrives in your inbox) that the universe is behind it all, smiling and cheering you along.

Chapter 4 Exercise

Noticing signs from the universe

Designate a page in your notebook to keep track of the signs and messages you receive from the universe as you journey down the path to your dream.

Everything counts: A nice email from a friend, a vivid dream, a poignant message scribbled on a bathroom wall. If it strikes you and stirs you it should go on your list.

Add signs you've received in the past to this list as well. That person you met who encouraged your dream? Add your encounter with him or her to the list. Assemble your list of signs from the universe. It's uncanny how many signs you will receive when you are open and willing to receive them.

_____

Chapter 5: Fear and obstacles

"If your dreams do not scare you they are not big enough."
–Ellen Johnson Sirleaf, President of Liberia

"I have accepted fear as a part of life- specifically the fear of change. I have gone ahead despite the pounding in the heart that says: turn back."
–Erica Jong, author and poet

Does the pursuit of your dreams terrify you? Are you scared? Welcome to the uncomfortable path that will lead you to your dreams. Fear and discomfort are a part of the package. Get used to their presence in your life.

One of the hardest things to come to terms with on this path is the undeniable and persistent presence of fear. Once we begin to walk towards our dreams, fear and doubt become a constant in our lives. At times we begin to question our decisions and our sanity.

The presence of fear is often misinterpreted as a red flag, a sign to back away and retreat to the comforts of the life we were living before. **Fear is not a red flag.**

Fear exists because there is no roadmap for what you are doing. The future is unknown, and that unknowable blank canvas is scary. If you are like me, you've spent most of your life on a very clear and well-trodden path. Perhaps you went to grade school, high school, and college. Maybe you went to graduate school. And then you got your first "real" job making photocopies at a law firm, working forty or fifty or sixty hours a week in order to make a good impression and position yourself to climb up the ladder. You were applauded for these efforts because they are the things you are supposed to do to get ahead. You followed the proverbial path. It was well lit and freshly paved and easy to navigate. And there were other people on the path with you so you didn't stand much chance of getting lost.

But now you have decided to veer from that path and fear has suddenly entered your life. Here you stand at the edge of a new path. This path is overgrown and littered with mud and weeds and rotting leaves. You know that a few people have turned down this path before but when you look down the path into the distance you don't see a soul before you. If you turn down this path you will be doing so alone.

Fear is standing next to you right now, whispering in your ear, telling you how risky it is to take this untrodden path. Fear is trying to convince you to stay on the path you are already on. "Be safe!" says fear. "You have no idea what will become of you if you leave this path. It isn't worth the risk." Fear does not want you to do something out of the ordinary. Fear hustles in favor of convention.

But here's the thing: Despite what Fear says, you *know* you are meant to take that path. You can't necessarily articulate why or how you know, but you know nonetheless. Still, fear is one persuasive bastard.

When I made the decision to leave my stable career to pursue my dream of writing I was terrified. I'd never been so scared in my life. I had to ask myself from time to time if I hadn't genuinely lost my mind. Because there was nothing in my life to indicate that I could actually make it as a writer. I wasn't even writing much! All I had to go on was that voice insisting that my life was not for living in a cubicle. I had to trust the deep, clear voice of my soul that begged me to follow my dreams.

Here is a short list of my fears at the time I decided to acknowledge my dreams:

I feared what my husband would think, what my parents would think, what my friends would think, what my co-workers would think. I feared losing health insurance, retirement and a paycheck. I feared I would fail. I feared I would never find a job again. I feared I would end up living on the streets. I feared I was going crazy. I feared that I was making an unfixable mistake. I feared I would fail as a writer. I feared that I would embarrass myself. I feared I would regret it.

Still, I moved forward.

The presence of fear does not mean that you should not move forward. Fear is just a fact in any colorful and unorthodox decision.

In many cases fear is actually a sign that you are on the right path because *big things are scary*. Meaningful things are scary. So try to become comfortable with the presence of fear in your life. Fear is normal. Fear is natural. Do not let fear stop you.

Living with fear

There is no trick to learning to live with fear. It's mostly about persistence. Acknowledge the presence of fear and move forward anyway. This will feel more comfortable with time, just as anything you practice becomes easier. And as you learn to live with fear you will find something else happening. As you move down the path towards your dream you will be very scared but you will also be gifted with moments of overwhelming joy and delight. As strong as that fear is, so will be your joy. As you take steps towards turning your dream into reality, you will find yourself feeling as though you are falling in love because you will be. You will be falling in love with the possibilities of your own life.

Do not expect fear to go away. Fear is here to stay. Eventually, once you have reached the other side of your dreams, you will find that the fear fades immensely, though it will never completely disappear. But that does not concern you now. Now, your task is to acknowledge the fear, know that it is normal, and try to become as comfortable as possible with it. Embrace it, even.

Overcoming obstacles

As you walk the path towards your dream you will encounter many obstacles. Some of these obstacles will be big and seem insurmountable. Some will be small and serve only to chip away at your self-confidence. Obstacles, like fear, just come with the territory.

When you encounter an obstacle, think of it as an opportunity to prove to yourself and the universe how badly you want to live your dream. Don't let an obstacle stop you.

Overcoming obstacles gives you confidence. Overcoming obstacles allows you to prove to yourself that you have what it takes to do the hard things. You learn that, while obstacles might set you back temporarily, nothing can stop you on your path to living your dreams. Obstacles are a blessing in disguise.

I encountered many obstacles (and still do!) on the path towards my dream. In my writing career, I am constantly faced with rejections and disappointments. Sometimes I feel as though I am failing more times than I am succeeding. But I do not let this stop me. I remind myself that this is just a part of the process. It does not matter how ugly and littered the path is. The only thing that matters is that we navigate the path to the end.

Expect obstacles. No matter what life puts in your way, keep walking.

There will be smooth parts on the path to your dream, too. Enjoy the moments when you make really good progress and you think, "This is getting easy!" But also know that those moments will not last (nothing lasts!).

What should you do when you hit a gigantic, seemingly insurmountable obstacle?

When you hit one of those gigantic, seemingly insurmountable obstacles, do not lose faith! The first thing to do is to take a step back. Sit with the obstacle for a few days. Take it all in. Know that just because you don't know how you'll get around the obstacle doesn't mean that there isn't a way around it, only that you haven't discovered the way yet.

Keep your eyes open for messages from the universe. They will come to you during the times when you need them most. The universe is on your side. The universe does not control the obstacles but the universe can point you in the direction of the path around them.

After you've sat with your obstacle for a few days you must begin to tackle it. Chances are that your time sitting with the obstacle brought you clarity and perspective. Maybe the obstacle doesn't even seem as big as it did a few days ago.

The first step towards tackling the obstacle is identifying the obstacle. What is it? Is it your own fear? Is it a family member who is unsupportive? Did something you were counting on fall through? Identify the components of the obstacle.

Now, start pecking at the obstacle like you're chipping at a block of ice. Once you begin chipping away at the obstacle you may find that it crumbles easier than you were expecting. You might find, once you have gotten close enough to the obstacle to touch it, that there is a path through the middle that you couldn't see from a distance.

Whatever the obstacle, remember that overcoming that obstacle is an opportunity to prove to yourself and the universe how badly you want to achieve your dream. When you get on the other side of this obstacle your confidence will soar. It is this belief in yourself and your abilities to take on even the hard things that will keep you marching towards living the life of your dreams.

———————

Chapter 5 Exercise

Getting around obstacles

Use this exercise when you encounter an obstacle on the path to your dream. At the top of a blank page in your notebook write the obstacle that you have encountered.

Underneath the obstacle list five ways in which you can get around the obstacle. For example, let's say that your car recently broke down and needs $1,000 in repairs. You are saving money to take a yearlong trip around the world. Spending $1,000 on your car is a major setback.

For this exercise you will write:

Obstacle: $1,000 car repair

Ways around the obstacle:

1. Work three extra weeks in order to replace the $1,000 I will be spending on the car.
2. Cancel cable (saves $100/mo.).
3. Search Craigslist for extra work. Pick up handyman and landscaping jobs on the weekends.
4. Sell my rarely used items in a garage sale.
5. Lower my trip budget by cutting out a stop on my itinerary.

No matter the obstacle you encounter, you will more easily overcome it when you have created an action plan to defeat it.

Chapter 6: Dealing with the naysayers

"Don't let the noise of other people's opinions drown out your own inner voice."
—*Steve Jobs, entrepreneur and inventor*

"One day you finally knew what you had to do, and began, though the voices around you kept shouting their bad advice."
—*Mary Oliver, poet*

No matter what your dream is, if it will take you off the well-worn path then you can count on one thing: you will encounter naysayers. And some of these naysayers may be very close friends or family and their opinion will matter a great deal to you.

In the beginning, the steps you take towards your dream may be so small that few people will notice them. Maybe you'll bring up a step in conversation, "You know, I really want to start painting again so I'm going to go out and buy some watercolor and brushes this weekend." And whoever you reveal this to will say, "That's wonderful!"

But as you continue to focus on your dream of painting, the dream will become bigger. It will begin to show up in your life in places that it did not exist before. You will begin to set aside time for your art. You will read more and talk more about it. Pieces of your life will shift and expand in order to make room for your art.

The naysayers will start piping up around this time.

When the same friend who encouraged you to buy watercolor paint and brushes asks you out to lunch a few months later, you might tell her that you aren't available because you've committed to painting on your lunch break. She may respond in a negative way, "Can't you just paint tomorrow?"

Many people close to you do want you to follow your dreams, but they don't want that dream to impact the relationship that they have with you already. Suddenly the dynamic of your relationship is shifting and those close to you may begin to resent your dream for interfering.

Naysayers come in many forms. Some may be outspoken and open in their views. Others may quietly oppose your dreams by avoiding them in conversation or changing the topic when they come up.

Most naysayers will be supportive to a point. However, if you are working towards something radical, they may be unsupportive from the get-go. Naysayers will tell you that you are being irresponsible. They will lay out all of the reasons that you should not go after your dream. They will make points that are hard to argue with: "What about your current responsibilities, your job, your retirement fund? What will you do if this doesn't work out?" And because you do not know the answers to these questions yet, they will use your inability to answer the questions against you. They will say, "Clearly this is just a spontaneous, undeveloped idea. Forget it."

In these moments you must remember that this dream has been growing inside of you for a long time. You have subconsciously and consciously been putting the puzzle pieces together inside of your soul. To the naysayer it may look as though you have just begun to follow your dreams, but in reality you know that you have been working on this for months or even years.

Seeing it from the naysayers point of view

It is hurtful when your mom or your best friend is less than supportive of the thing that means everything to you. You, on the other hand, have never been so excited. You wonder why the naysayer can't just be happy for you.

They're afraid of losing you, of course. They are worried that you will have your heart broken, that things won't work out as you hope they will. For most naysayers, their negativity originates from a place of love.

There may be an element of jealousy in their negativity as well. By making the big decision to open your own cupcake shop or move to France and study postmodern art, the naysayer feels that you have just pointed a big, blinking arrow at their own life. After all, if you can pursue your dream then that means that the naysayers can also pursue theirs. And chances are they aren't. Your unconventional decision feels to the naysayer like a judgment call on the decisions that they have made in their own lives.

As my husband and I were saving money so that we could pursue our traveling dream, he had a friend who would get upset when he would refuse to spend money. His friend would say, "Let's fly to California for a baseball game!" And my husband would say, "I'm sorry, I can't do that because I don't have the money." We were living on a very tight budget. But this friend knew how much money my husband and I had in the bank and could not understand why my husband just didn't spend some of that money on a fun weekend away with him. "You *do* have the money," his friend would say rather gruffly, "you are just refusing to spend it."

———————

Responding to the naysayers

It is best to respond to the naysayers closest to you with sensitivity and understanding. Like I mentioned above, they are afraid of losing you and they may also feel jealous. They are questioning their own decisions in life and your bold move might be bringing their old dreams to the surface. Try to explain to the naysayer why you are making the decisions you are making. Let them know how much your dream means to you and let them know how much their support means as well. Be sensitive to their feelings, but stay true to your dream. You can't control how the naysayers will respond to you, only how you will respond to them.

Some naysayers, however, you should cut out of your life completely. Toxic co-workers, friends that aren't ever there for you, family members that always leave you feeling drained. These people overtake you with their naysaying but don't bring anything positive to your life. Their negativity is just noise that does not do you any good. Keep your distance.

Support will come from unlikely places

The beauty of embracing and walking towards your dream is that the universe will continue to conspire for you. You will find as you walk this path that you will receive support from the most unlikely places and that a kind word or break in your favor will come just when you need it most.

Just as you are tackling the naysayers you will also find yourself amongst a small army of supporters. These people may be new to your life, new friends or peers that you have met while pursuing your dreams. These people will encourage you to continue down the path of your dreams. You will draw great strength from these supporters who can sympathize with your journey, many of them have taken a similar path.

A final thought on naysayers

Naysayers are an unavoidable part of this journey. Think of your most adamant naysayers as obstacles, road blocks in your path that allow you to prove to yourself and the universe how badly you want to live your dream.

Chapter 6 Exercise

Charting the naysayers

On a blank page in your notebook keep a list of naysayers currently in your life. Beside their names, make a note of how the naysaying manifests itself with that person. Does your Uncle Bill belittle your talents as an artist? Does your grumpy co-worker continually tell you that your plans to start your own business are futile?

Study the list. Which naysayers are key people in your life? Who can be avoided?

Chapter 7: Sacrifice

sac·ri·fice [sak-ruh-fahys]: The surrender or destruction of something prized or desirable for the sake of something considered as having a higher or more pressing claim.

"Figure out what your purpose is in life, what you really and truly want to do with your time and your life; then be willing to sacrifice everything and then some to achieve it. If you are not willing to make the sacrifice, then keep searching."
—Quintina Ragnacci, occupation unknown

I'm sure you've realized by now that your dream will require a tremendous amount of sacrifice. Just because you are doing the thing that means the most to you does not mean that it will come easy. In truth, the universe may ask you to give up a lot in order for you to step into your dream. Sacrifice is a part of this process, and it is another opportunity for you to prove to the universe how badly you want to do the thing that you were put on earth to do.

In order to live the full version of my dream, I had to give up my house, all of my possessions, my good job with my company-provided health insurance, my retirement account and my steady paycheck. There were no guarantees that my dream would ever be realized. I just sacrificed those things in faith that the life I wanted to live was possible.

The scary thing about making sacrifices for your dream is that you have to give up a lot. In many cases you must give up the things you have worked a lifetime for. But the secret behind these sacrifices is that you don't have to give up the things that really matter.

For instance, it was hard for my husband and I to sell our beloved house, but in the end we found that the freedom from a mortgage enabled us to save money to travel. It was hard for me to give up my paycheck, but I found that living without a steady income made me work harder than ever at establishing myself as a writer. Would I work so hard if I still had a steady paycheck? I don't think I would. The sacrifice is what propelled me towards the next step.

When you give so much up for your dream you will not just let your dreams fall by the wayside. You won't let a failure or two (or three!) keep you from continuing to pursue your dream. When you sacrifice you lay it all on the line, you invest everything, and this commitment will keep you going when times get tough.

Sacrifice is a necessary step on the path towards your dream. Sacrifice requires you to go all in. Put your chips on the table and bet on your dream.

Preparing to sacrifice

To truly sacrifice, you must prepare. I would not recommend leaving your office at 5 p.m. today, stopping by the art store, buying $25 worth of canvas and paint, and then calling into the office tomorrow with your resignation in order to fully commit to your dream of painting.

When I left my job to pursue my dream I did so after years of planning. My husband and I set a goal to save a certain amount of money, and we decide to use that money to travel while I simultaneously took a shot at writing. The money was our safety net, allowing us (we felt) to leave our jobs and take a stab at our dreams.

It took us three years to save this money and in that time we gave up so many things. We stopped shopping, we reduced our bills, we sold our car, and we paid off our credit cards. We said "no" to a lot of things because we couldn't justify the expense. All of those things were sacrifices but we were happy to make them because we were working towards our dream.

Planning for your dream may take years. You will have to commit to many small sacrifices, like saving money, before you dive in to your big sacrifices, like selling a house or leaving a job.

A friend of mine also had a dream of traveling the world. She worked *four jobs* for *three years* in order to pay off $25,000 worth of debt. When she'd paid off the debt she started saving her money in order to pursue her dreams of travel. This friend of mine was exhausted from juggling multiple jobs. She did not have a lot of time for relationships outside of her family. She was making major sacrifices and she struggled for a long time. But her sacrifices paid off. Now she has the freedom to live the life of her dreams.

Sacrifices can also be looked at as priorities. You give up one thing (the sacrifice) because you want another (to live your dream). Sacrifice is about figuring out what you want the most and then putting those things first in your life. Sacrifice is about making big and small decisions that align with the sort of life you want to live.

The good news about sacrifices

The good news about sacrificing is that, when you are making sacrifices in order to live your dream, most of the time they won't feel like sacrifices. Yes, I miss my blender.

I miss my closet full of clothes. I miss having a home. But never once have I thought to myself, "If only I could have that all back, what a terrible mistake I've made."

When you make sacrifices for your dream you may even feel a twinge of excitement because you know that the sacrifice you are making is bringing you one step closer to living your dream.

In these weeks, months and years building up to your dream you will make a lot of sacrifices. But when you are aligning your life up with your dreams, you will know that the sacrifices are all worth it. Remember that you will have to give things up and that it will be scary and painful at first. But rest assured that, when the time comes, you will be okay with it.

———————

Chapter 7 Exercise

What sacrifices will you need to make in order to live your dream?

On a blank sheet of paper in your notebook begin to make a list of the sorts of sacrifices that you will have to make in order to live your dream. For example, if your dream is to run a marathon, what are the sacrifices you will have to make in order to reach that goal? Your list might look something like this:

1. Give up my hour of TV after work in order to go for a run.
2. Get up early on Sunday mornings to complete long run before the weather gets too warm.
3. Cut back on eating out to only one night per week in order to control my diet.
4. Reduce unnecessary shopping in order to save money for marathon entry and travel expenses.
5. And so on…

———————

Chapter 8: Failure

"Just keep clear mind, go straight ahead, try, try, try for ten thousand years."
–Soen Sa Nim, Zen Buddhist master

"Courage does not always roar. Sometimes courage is the quiet voice at the end of the day saying, "I will try again tomorrow.""
–Mary Anne Radmacher, author and artist

I received an email once from someone who wanted to give me a reality check. The author of the email had sacrificed everything for his dream of owning land and running an organic farm. But the farm failed and the bank took his land away. He lost it all. "I just want you to know that this is the reality of my situation. I lost it all. My dream failed."

It's terrible when our dreams don't work out the way we think they should. But in these times we need to remember one very important thing: **We don't own the dream.** God owns the dream. We are just the conduits. We are the way that the dream lives in the world but we are not usually privy to the ways in which the dream will play itself out over time.

In other words, the universe knows more than we do. The man whose farm had failed believed that his dream had failed when in fact the only thing that had failed for this man was *his expected outcome* for his dream.

The loss of this man's property, the crumbling of his dream, was only the reality *of the moment*. His dream has only failed if he stops in the pursuit of it now. Life handed him one big obstacle, no doubt about that, but will it stop him? Perhaps the failure of his farm and the loss of his property were a necessary step in a grander vision for this man's life? In times of disappointment, we must remember that God knows more than we do.

Rethinking the concept of failure

What does it mean to fail? We generally describe failure as making an attempt at a goal and not achieving the desired result. But even if we don't achieve the result that we hope for we still achieve *some sort* of result, don't we? Our actions still lead us somewhere we wouldn't have been otherwise.

Failure is a way of looking at the world. If you write a book and try to land a book deal and you don't, perhaps you believe that you have failed. But you have not failed. You have changed the course of your life. You have written a book. You only fail if you stop now and leave the book that you've written lying dusty in your desk drawer never to be picked up again. If you keep working that book, if you make improvements and changes and then say, "What the hell, if I can't get a book deal I will just publish this thing myself," then you have not failed. You have succeeded in publishing your book even if it is in an alternative way than you originally envisioned. That's success, not failure.

I know this sounds hopeful and wildly optimistic and that the most skeptical of you will think, "Yeah, but that guy lost his farm. That's a crushing blow. How will he recover?"

It is a crushing blow. It is a terrible loss. We are never guaranteed success and we are certainly never guaranteed success on the terms in which we expect it.

Consider how many people fail before they succeed. How many people have started businesses that fail or had their farms shut down by the bank? How many artists have had their greatest works ripped to pieces? How many writers have had their stories rejected? In 1922, Hemmingway had his complete works stolen on a train. Paulo Coelho sold 900 copies of his first book. He wrote the second one anyway, because how could he not?

Failure, even a major one, should not stop you. Three failures should not stop you, thirteen should not. Learn from your failures. Perhaps the door to your dream slammed in your face, but did you see that other door down the hallway crack open? Failures, just like the voice that speaks inside of you, are messages from God. They're arrows that point towards the path to your most authentic dream. Remember that when failure strikes, and keep going, keep going, keep going.

Mistakes

You will make dozens (or hundreds!) of mistakes while walking the path to your dream. But just as failures are not really failures, mistakes are just necessary missteps that you need to take in order to meet success. You cannot reach your dream without making plenty of mistakes.

Each time you make a mistake consider yourself one step closer to your dream. A mistake is an experiment in which you reveal what *won't* work for you in order to bring yourself closer to all of the things that will. If you are making mistakes it means that you are pushing the boundaries of what you know how to do. When you make a mistake learn from it and then move forward. Do not dwell on the mistake. We all make them. We all need to make them.

The worthless trap of comparing ourselves to others

Many times, the feeling of failure is an illusion created by the dangerous and time-wasting trap of comparing ourselves to others.

If you want to be a writer you probably spend time reading all of the other people out there that also have the same dream as you do. The things that they write are funny and insightful and before long you find doubt creeping into your head. *I will never write like that*, you think. *I am not as talented as those writers. No one will want to read this useless crap I am writing.* Everyone around you seems to be landing book deals and getting full-spread articles in glossy magazines while you sit in your cheap apartment typing terrible stories on your computer and wandering around the kitchen to eat toast and pet the cat.

Remember this: **What other people do is of no concern to you.** The only thing of concern to you is your work and your dream. What matters now is that you do what you love, that you work towards the dream.

If you find yourself falling into the trap of comparing yourself to others, cut out the others. Get off of Facebook. Ban yourself from Twitter. Stop reading blogs and book reviews. It is okay to remove yourself from the game for a while. Lose the Internet and hole up in your bubble of safety and creativity. Exist for a while alone with your dream.

Remember, too, that you don't know the whole story. All

you are seeing are the most brag-worthy moments of other people's careers. You don't know how many times your peers were told "no" before the one time that they were told "yes."

_____

Remember, there is no such thing as failure

What a freeing thing to know! Even when that voice inside your head tells you that you have failed, let the voice inside of your soul remind you that there is no such thing as failure. Allow yourself the reassuring thought that you have followed your dream because you can't *not* follow it. Know that you do not know what the universe has in mind for you. Listen to the voice inside your soul and when something masquerading as failure strikes, as it ultimately will, know that this temporary failure is only one part of the longer journey towards your destiny.

_____

Chapter 8 Exercise

An incomplete list of failures

There is no such thing as failure. Still, many times we feel as though we have failed when what we are experiencing is nothing more than a diversion in our path.

On a blank piece of paper in your notebook make a list of ten past failures and what these failures lead to. For example, your list might look something like this:

Failure 1: I did not get the job I interviewed for and really wanted at Acme Company.

Outcome: Three months later I found a job that I love and that suits my skill set much better.

Failure 2: I did not get the role I auditioned for.

Outcome: I was devastated that I did not get the role. However, I did meet a new friend during the auditioning process that recommended me for a role in a play with a director I have always admired.

Failure 3: The launch of my online business flopped.

Outcome: I learned a lot from my failed business, including the importance of doing market research and creating a stellar business plan. My second business was a success because of the lessons I learned when my first business failed.

And so on...

Remember this list when you feel as though you are experiencing a failure. It will help you to see that the experiences that appear to be failures are bound to propel you in new and exciting directions. Eventually the reason for each of your "failures" will become clear.

———————

Chapter 9: Work like it means everything (because it does)

"We are what we repeatedly do. Excellence, therefore, is not an act but a habit."
—*Aristotle, philosopher*

"Great things are done by a series of small things brought together."
—*Vincent Van Gogh, painter*

We are all born with a specific purpose but that does not mean that the thing we are born to do will just fall into our laps. Even when we are following our destiny we must still work hard. We must work like it means everything, because it does.

Hard work is incredibly important. Hard work is what fills the space between achieving your dreams and just *dreaming* about them. All of the steps that we have covered so far in this book are important. It is important that you identify your dream. It is important that you listen to the voice that speaks from your soul. It is important that you notice the universe and deal with fear and obstacles and naysayers. But none of that matters much if you don't work hard. ***You must work hard.***

Hard work is important because it allows you to prove to yourself that you can do the thing that means so much to you. If you do not work hard you will not trust yourself. When you tell yourself, "I will work for three hours on my dream today by meditating, practicing yoga and journaling," but life gets in the way and you never get around to working on your dream, then you have let yourself down. And over time, if you let yourself down too often, you will begin to believe that you cannot be trusted to do the work to achieve your dream.

You have to uphold the promises you make to yourself through hard work. Doing so builds confidence.

As I mentioned in Chapter 3, when I was in my early 20's I was very overweight. I eventually lost 80 pounds and became a marathon runner. When I decided to lose weight I knew that I had to give everything to that goal. I turned down dinner invitations and happy hours because they would break my diet. I went to the gym every day, even when I didn't want too, even when it was rainy or cold or early or late and I didn't feel like leaving my apartment. I went when I had a headache and I went when I was rushed and I went when I was tired. I went *every single day*. And through that commitment I learned that I would show up for myself. I learned that I could be trusted. I learned that I was the sort of person that could see something through to the end. I didn't know this about myself at the beginning. I am certain that learning this is what planted the seeds of confidence to follow my biggest dreams of writing and seeing the world.

Hard work trumps almost everything. You do not need to be the most talented person in the world. You do not need to write like Ernest Hemmingway or Virginia Woolf. You need to write like you and then you need to work hard. Hard work will make up for whatever you might lack in talent. Talent will only take you so far; hard work will take you the rest of the way.

The importance of play

Chances are your dream requires you to be creative or to express yourself. Maybe your dream is to work in the arts or maybe your dream is to start a Fortune 500 company.

Maybe you dream of opening a cupcake shop or becoming a professional dog walker. Whatever it is that you dream of, it will require creative thinking. And creativity requires play. It is incredibly important that you make room in your life for play. This will help you grow exponentially in the direction of your dreams.

Those of us who are comfortable with hard work tend to overwork. We feel like we are never doing enough, that we should be working longer and harder in the pursuit of our dreams. We work until we've drained ourselves and then we keep working. We tap into our reserves and drain those too. We burn ourselves out.

This is where the importance of play comes in. We must set boundaries on our work and schedule time to play. Play will restock our shelves of creativity. Playing revives our energy and enables us to work better.

There is plenty of time to work. But in order to reach our dreams we must remember that there is also time to play. Play is a component of hard work.

Commitment

Fully committing yourself to your dream is not an easy thing to do. You will encounter tremendous resistance from yourself and from those around you. The naysayers will be barking at your door. But truly committing means that you have removed your head as a barrier to your dream. No matter how much your head whines and begs you to just watch *American Idol* instead, you sit yourself down in a quite place and draw for an hour. Honor your commitment.

Think about a successful person who is living a version of

your dream. How did they get to where they are today? We so often see a successful person but forget to consider what it took for them to get to where they are. We do not think of the mornings they spent working on their novel, at 5 a.m., before the kids got out of bed. We do not hear about all of the rejection letters, all of the times they were told no. We do not see that before the success there was hard work and a commitment to the dream no matter what sort of obstacles were thrown onto their path.

A bit about excuses

Let's just get this out of the way: Excuses are bullshit. Everyone on the planet can come up with a million reasons why they can't make concerted efforts towards their dreams. You can't get in shape because you don't have the time to exercise or you can't afford a gym membership or you have a slow metabolism. Listen, the world doesn't need any more excuses, so save your breath.

There's just no such thing as a valid excuse. You have kids so you can't write, you have a job with long hours so you can't exercise, you have a partner that doesn't support your study of Reiki and so you aren't going to find a teacher. It's all true, I know, but it's also all bullshit. If you are absolutely 100% committed to your dream *you will find a way.*

Excuses are convenient reasons to avoid your dream. We use excuses because we fear failure or rejection or what the naysayers will say. We use excuses because we fear ourselves. We fear the brilliancy of our own potential. We fear what we could become. We fear totally changing our lives and leaving the security blanket of the status quo behind.

When you make an excuse you are essentially declaring to the universe that you will not own your decision to follow your dream. By removing yourself from the equation and blaming an external force, you are giving yourself an exit strategy. You are setting up your life so that, if things don't turn out as you hope, you do not have to stand front and center and own what happened. With your safety net of an excuse you can say, "Oh, the reason it didn't turn out the way I wanted it to is because my family wasn't supportive."

When you make excuses you rob yourself of the pleasure of true commitment.

In order to reach your full potential you have to own your decisions. It's so important to do this. Because when you own your decision, even when it is a bad one, you know that above all else you will be honest with yourself and take responsibility for your own actions. But when you use an excuse you send a message to your soul that you do not trust it.

You have to trust and believe in yourself. If you do not trust or believe in yourself you will succumb to the naysayers and the fear and the doubt and all of the other monstrous things that will try to drag you away from your dream. You have to be certain about your integrity. If you are not certain about your integrity right now *that is okay*, but now is the moment to begin to be certain. Right now, this instant, find one thing to commit yourself to. Commit to writing one page in your journal every single day for the next week. Commit yourself to getting out into nature for a walk once a week. Whatever your dream is, find one thing that will propel you down the path towards it and commit yourself to it. Do it no matter what, no excuses this time. You need these small victories. The small victories piled on top of one another eventually serve to show you that you are capable of big things.

Kristin Armstrong, a runner and the ex-wife of Lance Armstrong, said this about working hard and committing to a dream: "It's who you are when no one is watching that builds the confidence to give your best in the moments when it's time to be seen."

You are at the beginning of your journey right now. There aren't too many people watching. In fact, maybe you are the only person who knows that you are on your journey. Work hard. Commit yourself and stick with it. Prove to yourself that you can do hard things.

Chapter 9 Exercises

Introducing play back into your life

What do you like to do for fun? What makes you feel lighthearted and free? What makes you laugh?

Create a list of the things that bring the feelings of joy and freedom into your life. Does hiking make you happy? Does dancing bring you joy? Does playing flag football with your brothers or baking cookies or going to the movies always bring a smile to your face?

Play is an important part of refilling the stores of creativity inside of you. Play enables you to work hard. Keep this list of play at hand and try to do at least one of the things on your list each week.

Small victories

It is impossible to overestimate the importance of setting and conquering small, achievable goals. Reaching these goals allows you to prove to yourself that you are committed to your dream.

Take out your notebook and write at the top of a blank page: This week's five achievable goals.

Underneath list five goals that you can accomplish within the next seven days. These goals do not need to relate to your dream at all. They only serve to prove that you will hold yourself to the commitments you make.

Here is a sample list of small, achievable goals:

- Monday: Walk the dog for twenty minutes
- Tuesday: Wash the dish cloths
- Wednesday: Write in my journal
- Thursday: Call my sister just to say hello
- Friday: Eat a healthy breakfast

The goals can be small and seemingly meaningless. They take on meaning when you commit yourself to meeting them.

———————

Chapter 10: You have the tools

"Everything you can imagine is real."
–Pablo Picasso, artist

"You are never given a dream without also being given the power to make it come true."
–Richard Bach, writer

When you begin to wonder whether you really have the talent or ambition to accomplish your dream, remember this: **You already have all of the tools you need to make your dream come true.**

As you begin to walk the path to your dream you will find that you are stronger and more resourceful than you know. When you begin to live a life that is more authentic the best parts of you begin to emerge.

Human beings are so powerful. We have the capacity to do the most amazing things. So what stops us all from being the powerhouses of talent and success that we are capable of being? Doubt stops us. Fear stops us. We stop ourselves and get in our own way.

This quote by Marianne Williamson, a spiritual author and lecturer, has become something of an anthem for those of us pursuing our dreams:

"Our deepest fear is not that we are inadequate. Our deepest fear is that we are powerful beyond measure. It is our light, not our darkness, that most frightens us. We ask ourselves, Who am I to be brilliant, gorgeous, talented, fabulous? Actually, who are you not to be? You are a child of God. Your playing small does not serve the world. There is nothing enlightened about shrinking so that other people

won't feel insecure around you. We are all meant to shine, as children do. We were born to make manifest the glory of God that is within us. It's not just in some of us; it's in everyone. And as we let our own light shine, we unconsciously give other people permission to do the same. As we are liberated from our own fear, our presence automatically liberates others."

In my case, I've always known that I wanted to write, but I didn't believe that I had the talent to be a writer. I was afraid of my own light. I was afraid to find out how brightly I could shine.

Who decides what sort of talent we have? I spent too many years putting emphasis on what my peers were creating and what my teachers thought. It was paralyzing. And then one day a radical idea came to me: *If you want to be a writer, Kim, then write.* Talent doesn't make you a writer. Teachers don't make you a writer. Hanging out with writers doesn't make you a writer. Writing makes you a writer.

I had all of the tools inside of me to start writing. I already had everything I needed. I was the only thing holding me back.

Just imagine that when you were born God packaged you up and imprinted on your soul the unique thing that you are needed on earth to do. Then He (or She or It, depending on what God is to you) made sure that you had all of the tools to do it. He put that voice inside your soul so that He could always communicate with you, and you with Him. He couldn't guarantee that life on earth wouldn't interfere with His plans. He does not control human decisions after all. But He sent you down to earth with all of the tools you need to fulfill your purpose, just like a mother packs a backpack full of supplies for her child on the first day of kindergarten. You showed up here on earth with everything you need, but it's up to you to take those crayons out of the box and draw.

―――――――――

Name what you are

I remember when I ordered my first set of business cards for my blog. They said:

Kim Dinan, Writer

Oh my God I was thrilled to see my name on paper next to the title *Writer*. But I was also terrified to hand those cards out. I feared that once I claimed to be a writer I would be judged on my skill as a writer. Other people would see that I called myself a writer and think, *Who does she think she is, proclaiming herself a writer? Does this girl actually think she can write?* In the beginning, I was ashamed. I felt like a fraud. I felt I should preface my declaration of writer with a disclaimer: "Well, just so you know, I'm not *really* a writer. I only write in my free time. I just have this tiny blog…"

Here's what I eventually learned: No one cared. The thing I'd failed to realize during my internal freak-out about calling myself a writer was that the universe does not revolve around me! Most people couldn't care if I called myself a writer or a tax attorney or a professional bubble blower. What I am, the identity that I feel and wanted to share with the world, only mattered to me. That realization set me free.

Being a writer matters to me and being *called* a writer matters to me. The names that we use for ourselves matter. Maybe you are an actress that hasn't stepped onto the stage since your third grade rendition of *Snow White and the Seven Dwarfs*. Who cares? If you know inside that you are an actress, if being a part of the theater makes you feel like every atom in your body is zinging and sparking with life, than that is exactly what you are. You are an actress. Go find your stage.

Seeing your toolbox

Think about someone that you love and adore. Perhaps it's a child, either your own or a niece or nephew. Perhaps it is a sibling or a partner in life. It doesn't matter who it is, just think of that person in your head.

It feels nice to focus on someone you love, doesn't it?

Now, think about how much confidence you have in this person that you love. Think about how you know that they are capable of anything they put their mind to. Think about how you have the upmost confidence that their abilities are limitless and that they are filled with an earth-shattering amount of intelligence. Think about their natural ability, how you have seen them surprise themselves over and over again, but that their achievements never surprise you because you know how capable and talented this person is. Think about how you *know* that this person has everything it takes to make their dreams come true.

Now, know that this person is **you.** The capability for success that you see in the person you love is not *only* in the person you love. It is in you too. It is in every single one of us. We all have the tools.

As the introductory quote to this chapter reminds us, we are not given a dream without also being given the tools to make it come true. If you can dream it, you can accomplish it. You have all the tools you'll ever need to make your dreams come true. Believe in your toolbox.

The exercises are a part of your toolbox

I hope that you have been completing the exercises at the end of the chapters in this book. The notebook that you have been using to complete the exercises is an important tool in your toolbox.

Throughout the course of this book you have assembled the tools for your toolbox by describing your dream, giving your soul room to speak, identifying signs from the universe, creating a list of ways to be playful, identifying what you are naturally good at, seeing the other side of failure, assembling a list of concrete actions you can take towards your dream, and gathering the tools to move past obstacles and deal with negativity and naysayers in your life. Use the tools in your toolbox as often as possible, they will help you down the path towards your dream.

Chapter 11: Identifying success

"A jug fills drop by drop."
–Buddha, sage and founder of Buddhism

"The price of success is hard work, dedication to the job at hand, and the determination that whether we win or lose, we have applied the best of ourselves to the task at hand."
–Vince Lombardi, American football coach

In Chapter 8 we learned that there is no such thing as failure, just various ups and downs on the path towards ultimately fulfilling your dream. We've learned a lot about "failure," but what does success look like?

I love the quote by Buddha, "A jug fills drop by drop," because the only way to realize your dream is drop by drop. And each drop in your jug is a success.

Spend a moment thinking about your dream. Now think about what success looks like as it relates to your dream. How will you know when you have achieved your dream? When will you know that you've "made it"? Go back in your notebook and look at the first exercise we did way back in the preamble of this book. Read again the description of what the perfect day living the life of your dreams looks like.

When we start out down the path to our dream we have an idealized version of that dream in our head. As we begin to walk the path towards realizing the dream, we begin to see that our dream is messy and complicated. Our dream will not look like what we imaged it would look like. Success will not look like what we imagine it to look like either.

Success is a relative term. To the rest of the world, making a small salary as a writer might not be the pinnacle of success. For me, however, it means that I get to do what I love and earn enough money to live a simple but fulfilling existence. I am not making six figures a year but I am doing what I love and I believe that I have found success. Because I am ambitious I want my success to grow and continue, but I make it a point to regularly stop and acknowledge the fact that I have successfully reached my initial dream. We will talk more about the evolution of dreams and goals in the next chapter.

Just as we tend to misidentify temporary setbacks as permanent failure, we also tend to put too much stock in our first successes. We will have ups and downs on the long road to achieving what we want. Just as we cannot allow ourselves to lose the path when an obstacle enters our field of vision, we also cannot expect one success to lead to another. When you have a success, and another drop lands in your jug, celebrate it! But know that there will be times in the future when your jug will leak as well. Keep an even keel when possible and remember that the path to your dream will more closely resemble a roller coaster ride than a stroll through an open meadow.

Sniffing out success

We so often have an idea of what success looks like in our heads that we do not recognize it when it comes to fruition in our lives. We think that we will be successfully fit when we have lost twenty-five pounds, that we will be a successful artist when our first piece goes to auction for thousands of dollars, that we will be a successful musician when we hit the top ten charts, a successful business owner when we have franchised into four locations across town. We think of success as a destination that we must arrive at, as one crowning moment of achievement or nothing at all.

I started my blog *So Many Places* because I wanted to write, simple as that. I knew what my passion was, my calling in life, but I did not know how to begin. So I started a blog and decided to carve out my own little space on the Internet. My blog gave me a place to come to write and to hone my voice.

For a year or more no one read my blog. My mom didn't even read my blog. But I didn't think of myself as failing, though I'm sure to most people it probably looked like I was. I was writing and I was happy writing and when someone would comment on my blog the thrill of knowing that I was writing for someone other than myself felt like a success, and it was.

I counted each page view as a success, each comment as a success. I considered each blog post that I published as a success, because I was taking the time out of my busy 9-5 life to focus on what I loved. I was finally writing when before I was only *dreaming* of writing. Each word on the page was a tiny little explosion of success.

If everyone in the world defined success as having a New York Times bestselling book, a corporation that employs thousands of people, or paintings hanging in the Metropolitan Museum of Art, there would be very few successful people in the world.

Success is doing what you want to do, what you love and what makes you come alive. If you are doing those things, that jug that Buddha speaks of is already more than halfway filled. It is important to remember that success might not look like you expect it to look when it knocks at your door but, still, you must learn to identify it and invite it to come in.

———————

Chapter 12: The evolution of your dream

"We must look for ways to be an active force in our own lives. We must take charge of our own destinies, design a life of substance and truly begin to live our dreams."
—Les Brown, musician and composer

"To want to be what one can be is purpose in life."
—Cynthia Ozick, writer

As you walk down the path towards your dream something will become clear to you. You will see that your dream has morphed and changed. Dreams evolve over time.

My dream, as you are well aware by now, was to write for a living and travel.

Today, I have traveled the world for two years (and I am still traveling) and I have a widely read blog that provides income, as well as freelance work and a job speaking for a magazine. I've also published this book. For all intents and purposes I have achieved my original dream. In fact, if you'd told me three years ago that I would be traveling the world and making a small but steady income writing and speaking I would have been thrilled.

But that doesn't mean that I am now kicked back on the beach in Indonesia with a cocktail in my hand (okay, I am). I didn't just reach the original version of my dream and then stay there. I still have dreams that I am working towards. I reached my *original* dream, but as I continued down the path towards achieving my dream it continued to evolve.

The dream you have now is just the beginning of something very big. Your dream will change and grow over time into something even more than it is now. There is something behind your original dream, waiting to be revealed, but you won't see what it is until you reach the first iteration of your dream.

You can't predict how you dream will evolve. You may be surprised when you notice one day that you are yearning for something that wasn't originally included in the design of your dream. Stay open and let your dream grow. You will begin by taking the first step, and then the second step, and then the third. As each step appears before you, you will notice subtle changes in your dream.

Because of a dream's tendency to grow, it is important to keep yourself open to the changes as they arise. Right now your dream might be to open an art gallery. As you take steps down this road you may realize that your true passion is to bring art to a sector of the public that doesn't generally have access to it. You assumed your dream was to open an art gallery because an art gallery was an obvious way of sharing art with the public. But as you continued to walk the path, and as your dream evolved, you began to find opportunities and outlets for sharing art with the public that you never knew existed before. By starting on the path to your dream you were introduced to a number of opportunities that were not clear at the beginning of your path, and because of this you are able to redefine what your dream looks like.

Think of the evolution of your dream as perfecting a recipe. You know you want to bake a cake. You start out with the ingredients and a recipe. You add the ingredients together. You bake the cake. It's good, but something is missing. The next time you add cinnamon to give the cake more flavor. You add an extra teaspoon of vanilla to sweeten the cake. Always, you are perfecting the recipe, adding ingredients and subtracting others, working towards the best possible version.

When I started down the path to my dream I knew, very simply, that I wanted to travel and write. I didn't know how to do that or what it would look like. So I started saving money to travel and I started writing. I picked up my journal again. I started a blog. And over time I found that what interests me about writing are the same things that interest me about life: I love the small details and the connections we have to each other. I love exploring the emotions that connect us all around the world.

I had no idea that my little travel blog, which I started just so that I could simply *write,* would morph into a place where I could explore my greater love of the world and our connections to it, but it did. I have been able to refine my calling by starting with that first step: My desire to travel and write.

As I have continued on my path my vision has become clearer. I started working on a travel memoir. I wrote this little book and am working on others. I never would have guessed that these projects were in my future. My dream evolved and brought me here. I know my dream will keep evolving in the future and your dream will evolve too.

———————

In closing: Be on fire

"The most powerful weapon on earth is the human soul on fire."
–Ferdinand Foch, French solider and writer

A few months ago while I was in Nepal, I was talking with a paraglider who told me that as he is floating up in the sky, catching currents of wind and flying like a bird, he'll steer his glider so that it is hovering over a single person walking along the road hundreds of feet below.

He told me that he does this because even a single person can create a current of energy that he can catch to push his glider up towards the clouds. This is how I know that the energy of a single person shifts the atmosphere on earth.

When you commit yourself to following your dream the world will shift. It will shift for you and it will shift for those around you. And as you continue walking down the path towards your dream, encountering obstacles and then overcoming them, the energy around you will build. It will grow stronger and you will pull people towards you. They will want to know what you are doing. They will want to know your secret. They will want to know why they leave you feeling like anything is possible. And you will know that it is because you have finally admitted that the possibilities for your life are endless. When you live your truth you enable other people to feel the truth inside of themselves as well.

The path to your dream will be long and it will change as you change. But the second you take those first steps, which may be as simple as reading this book, you have changed the course of your life. You take one step and then another and over time you will be transformed. You have your dream now and it is in your head, a perfect version of your dream, but it will not turn out as you expect it to. In fact, it may turn out even bigger and more brilliant than you are able to imagine now. Sometimes our dreams and our beliefs in ourselves are not as big as what is possible for our lives. As you grow and work on your dream, you will find that the expectations and possibilities of your life will grow too.

I am not an expert on these things. I am simply one person who decided to live my dream and has been bowled over by the possibilities of life once I started living the way I was meant to live. And I have seen the same transformation in others. When you are on the right path there is no limit to how far you can go. When you answer the voice of your soul and follow your dream it will make you feel as though your life is on fire.

I hope for you a life on fire. It is not just possible for me or for your neighbor or your sister. It is not just possible for the most talented and brilliant among us. It is possible for every single one of us, including you. It is possible because you have dreamed it. It is possible because it is the truth that the voice inside your soul speaks. And you would not have been given your dreams and that voice if it was not possible for the things that you dream to come true.

Extend your hand.

Strike the match.

Live on fire.

About the author

In May 2012, American writer Kim Dinan and her husband left their 9-5 jobs, sold their possessions, and set out into the world to write and travel. Today, Kim is a full-time traveler and writer whose work has been featured in national and International magazines and in major online publications such as the Huffington Post. Her popular blog so-many-places.com has chronicled her journey since the beginning. You can get in touch with her anytime via email at kim@so-many-places.com.

Made in the USA
San Bernardino, CA
08 November 2016